SCARLESS

A WOMAN'S JOURNEY TO FINDING STRENGTH AND IDENITY

KANISHA ANTHONY

Printed in the United States of America

First Printing, 2018

ISBN 978-0692070833

www.KanishaAnthony.com

ACKNOWLEDGEMNETS

I would like to give special thanks, to all those who made my book writing successful and assisted me at every point to cherish my goal.

First and foremost, I want to thank God, for none of this would be possible with out his grace.

To my husband, my rock, my safe place. For his constant love and support and always pushing me to conquer my goals.

To my children, whom I hope always know how much they are a blessing to me. Thank you for giving me a reason to never give up.

To my friend, my sister, my mentor, Nikki. Thank you for believing in me even when I didn't believe in myself. This book would not yet be done without your encouragement and time you put in to assist me. And to all my family and friends (old and new) who encouraged me on this journey, who listened to me cry, and always gave a helping hand, thank you. My life would not be complete without you.

Dedication

This book is dedicated to the two brave police officers who risked their lives to save mine. I cannot express my gratitude enough for the service you provided.

Thank you.

Contents

INTRODUCTION

FROM THE EYES OF THE SAVIOR'S

About a year ago I came across this story which brought back lots of memories and inspired me at the same time. It was the story of two police officers who witnessed first-hand, the ravaging havoc a fire disaster can do. My heart broke a thousand times as they recounted how they risked their lives in the bid to save the life of two children, but despite all their efforts, the burning inferno proved that it was stronger.

In the story, Wentzville police officer Keith Cummins recalled the exact time he arrived at the burning house on Nov 24 at 8:54 am. It was a beautiful morning, the streets were alive with people going to their work places, and school busses filled with school children. For the rest of the world, that fateful day was just like every other week day, but for Cummings and police Sgt. Harry Belcher, it was the day they had no other choice than to pull an act of bravery which made them become heroes and won them many awards and recognitions all over the state.

There was a huge fire outbreak at the house on 1400 block of Plaza Street. The occupant of the house, Deadra McDaniel had escaped the fire with one of her children and was across the street when the police arrived. Her two sons, six years old Travis, and Marcus who was only two years old died in the fire. Her four-year-old daughter, Kanisha was seriously wounded, and is hospitalized with severe burns on over 36 percent of her body.

It was the day before Thanksgiving; Cummins was in his patrol car near the intersection of Pearce Boulevard and Highway 61, when the fire was reported over his police radio. From his position, he could see a heavy cloud of smoke billowing.

"When I got there, the two front bedrooms were fully engulfed and I could see smoke coming out the front door," he said.

As he got out of his patrol car, neighbors yelled, "There are children in the house!"

Cummins ran into the house, which was now filled with smoke and fire. He tried to crawl to the back bedroom where two children had been sleeping, but the fire was so hot that and forced Cummins back outside. He asked one of the neighbors for a wet towel to cover his head. Again, he attempted to go inside the house, but the inferno thickened, and he couldn't go far inside the house before he staggered out, coughing and wheezing, with the rings of thick cloudy smoke he had inhaled wafting out from both his nose and mouth.

At that moment, Sgt. Harry Belcher arrived. Although Cummins was choking on the smoke, he managed to tell Belcher about the children in the burning house.

"I went into the house and made an attempt to get back to the bedroom where the children were," said Belcher. "The only real thing on my mind was how to get those children out of there."

The fire and smoke also forced him outside.

"It was just one huge ball of fire," said Belcher.

When he got back outside, the neighbors told both policemen that there was a little girl in the bedroom near the front.

Belcher broke the window with his hand and dived into the room, and Cummins held onto his feet so he would be able to pull him out of the fire.

The smoke was so thick that Belcher could not see anything. "Give me a flashlight," he yelled, and then Cummins handed him a flashlight.

As he moved the light around the room, he spotted the child's foot. He grabbed the foot and was able to put his other hand under the child's back.

He yelled for Cummins to pull him out of the room. With Cummins pulling his leg, Belcher pulled the little girl, Kanisha out of the house. Some moments later, the ambulance arrived.

"She was unconscious," said Belcher. "When they got her in the ambulance a few minutes later, they confirmed that she was alive."

At the end of the day, the officers were unable to save the two boys in the house; Cummins was hospitalized for smoke inhalation, and Belcher was treated for lacerations to his hand.

The two officers have been honored by the Police Department and by Mayor Darrel Lackey for their efforts to save the children.

Perhaps the most prestigious award received by the officers was the Distinguished Service Awards presented by the Board of Governors for Law Enforcement Officials of St. Louis. The awards, never given before to officers outside of St. Louis County, are the organization's highest honor, and only a few are presented each year.

Both officers are modest about the

praise, saying the neighbors should be credited for aiding in the rescue efforts.

"I just think the neighbors did a heck of a job," said Cummins. "They were fighting the fire when we got there."

The house was equipped with a smoke alarm, but it was not working because the batteries were dead. The mayor has asked police officers to carry batteries with them on patrol and install them for residents who need new batteries in their smoke detectors.

Belcher hopes the batteries will prevent more deaths in house fires.

For Belcher, the recognition follows a year of emotional upheaval. He was fired from the Police Department last December. He fought the firing and was reinstated after the April election changed the makeup of the Board of Aldermen. He was later honored by fellow city employees by being selected "Employee of the Year."

"It's been crazy," said Belcher. "I've had a combination of the happiest and the saddest year."

Perhaps what makes Belcher the saddest is thinking about the children lost in the fire.

"I feel sorry we weren't able to do anything for the little boys," said Belcher. "I worry about the little girl and how she'll be. I know she'll have to go through a long recovery."

This was the article I found when I when I was curiously researching prior to writing my story. As I read this story, streams of tears rolled down my face. At that moment, it brought back one of the only memories I had from that day.

You see, after I was taken to the hospital, there were a few minutes in which my heart stopped beating. It was exactly two to three minutes. In those two to three minutes, I had what I would call an encounter with God.

To paint a clearer picture, I saw a blue background and in front of me were two huge white wings. They were wings of an angel, but I heard a voice, and that voice said to me loud and boldly, "Kanisha I must take your brothers with me. They are in a safe place, but for you, I have something special waiting at home for you."

Until this day, those words sit in my mind and remind me just how grateful I am. Grateful to God and grateful to those officers he sent to save me. In this book, I share with you trials and tribulations I went through as a burn survivor- the good, the bad, and the amazing.

CHAPTER 1

THE ROAD TO RECOVERY

When I say that my whole life is an expression of God's grace. You may not understand it until I tell you how God raised me from the dead, and brought me back to life when everyone else, including the doctors had given up on me. After that infernal fire almost burned me to death, I was left in the mercy of the doctors. The doctors did all they could to save me, but even as they struggled, they were so convinced that their efforts would not yield any fruits.

There I was, lying in a hospital bed wrapped up with white bandages from head to toe like an Egyptian mummy of ancient times. Almost all the organs in my body had gone dead, so I had tubes inserted down my throat, some to help pass air down my lungs, and others to put food inside my body. It all made me feel like an inanimate object and I so badly wanted to pull them out, but I couldn't even blink, talk, or move my arms or legs. I couldn't understand what was happening to me; I tried to open my mouth to talk to my family, who surrounded my bed, but nothing came out. I could hear them, but they couldn't seem to hear me.

I tried to force myself to speak, but after

trying for so many minutes, I gave up. That is when I overheard the conversation one of the doctors were having with my grandmother. The doctor explained to her that this was going to be my last surgery. I had been having surgeries every week, and the surgeries didn't seem to be helping at all. The doctor didn't sound excited or optimistic about the surgery. The doctor would rather let me be the way I was, so I could die peacefully without going through the pain of their mutilating knives again, but I guess their choices were tied to medical ethics, so they just needed to do it anyway.

He, however, prepared every one of my family members to prepare their minds to see me in a vegetative state, because it seemed like that was the place I was going to live the rest of my life.

It was obvious that the doctors were deciding to give up on me. "This can't be happening to me," my tender spirit cried. "This is not what God wants for me." Though I was a little child, the flight I was going through was fast making me spiritually matured. I was trying to hold on to life with every ounce of strength in me, and even though everyone else was resigning to fate, I was crying for mercy, for God to work out a miracle for me somehow.

And right then, I saw two big fluffy angel wings.

Even after twenty-something years later I can still remember it, as clear as day. The wings were beautiful and it seemed like they were floating right before me, and within a moment, I saw myself floating with the angel wings.

That was when I heard a voice that I will never forget. It was a deep yet calming voice, and it said in these exact words: "My daughter I had to take your brothers with me but they are in a safe place. I have something special waiting at home for you."

It was simple and sweet, nothing more, nothing less.

Back then I didn't really understand, I was only 4 years old, but I knew that it was the voice of God that spoke to me.

God showed himself to me in a vision when my heart stopped. People must have thought that my life was over, but in the spirit, I was having a divine encounter with God. It was a life-changing encounter, during which God showed and told me that he had a purpose for my life. He proved to me that what I was going through, and what I was about to go through, had deep-seated meanings attached to them. From that day until today, I have come to realize that God does not put us through anything without having a purpose behind it.

I shared that story with my family once I was able to talk. Out of the mouth of a baby, sharing that I had an encounter with God, put everyone in a state of awe.

It was amazing because I didn't know much about God. I mean, at that age all I was worried about was dolls and cartoons. So, for me to speak those words out of my mouth they knew it was true and they knew it was God.

After that last surgery, which the doctors performed without any hope of getting a positive result, the doctors all finally declared that there was nothing else could be done for me. I was so badly burned on the top of my head that it had taken off the first 3 layers that were protecting my scalp and was causing the brain's functionality to go downhill.

"We did the best that we could do." explained the doctor as he rolled me into the recovery room. "She is still out from the surgery, and when she wakes up it would be a miracle if she could function halfway we normally do."

A miracle it was! I not only woke up halfway functioning, I woke up fully functional. I opened my eyes, tried to lift my head and said, "Can I have a glass of milk please?"

Go ahead have a praise break! This is definitely a praise break kind of moment! Shout hallelujah as loudly as your voice can go! Only God deserves the praise for this kind of miracle.

The doctors were speechless, they had no idea how something like this could be happening.

The four-year-old little girl who once laid on that hospital table with no heartbeat, the little girl with a brain that couldn't function for weeks, had awakened from the surgery that potentially was supposed to do nothing, and was up smiling and talking. "Jesus Christ!" I could imagine even the staunchest atheist amongst them shouting.

When I got older my grandmother explained to me that her church held a special service for me that morning of the surgery. It was a Sunday, but for them, it wasn't like any other Sunday. That day they canceled all the normal things they usually do in service and instead decided to spend many hours praying for me.

Talk about the power of Prayer! I was lying down almost like a vegetable, men had given up, but the church was there interceding for me. Now that I think of it, I have come to realize that there is absolutely no problem that is too hard for God to solve. I believe because of their prayers, because of their voices ringing loud to the gates of heaven that God sent that angel to come and keep me under those protective wings. A saying *"When man works, man works; but when man prays, God works."* Their prayers stirred God into action. He moved in swiftly and delivered me from the hands of death, and from that day, everyone who saw me called me a miracle child.

I still have notes of people saying that they prayed for me; and letters from strangers saying that they put angels all over their homes after hearing my story.

Have you ever been through a time in life where you felt like everything was going downhill? Have you ever been in a situation where you question God and asked him why this was happening to you?

Maybe everything was going great in life and all of a sudden things changed and people told you-you were not going to make it through this.

I believe we all go through these moments. We all have battles and storms that we face in life; but we also all have a purpose, each and every one of us. God does not put anyone on this planet without designing a purpose for their lives.

I need you to answer this question sincerely; have you survived every single storm that you have been through in life? If you are reading this the answer is yes. I say so because if you didn't survive, then you wouldn't be alive at this very moment, reading this book.

Every super awful, horrible and crappy day that you have come across, counts for one storm or the other, but you somehow managed to survive them all. You know what this says about you? It says that you are stronger than you think.

The next time you are having a rough day and you aren't quite sure how you will survive it, remember you have survived every single bad day so far and you can survive this one. All you need to do is believe in God, hold fast on every one of His promises, and convince yourself that God has a plan for you; a plan not to make those storms consume you, to make you come out victorious on the other side of the deep sea in which you have found yourself.

KANISHA ANTHONY

CHAPTER 2

GRACE BEYOND PAINS

The hospital became a place that I had learned to like. It was a place that didn't seem too bad, even on the days when I was in excruciating pain. Day after day I would have to get my dressings changed. Getting your dressings changed doesn't sound like such a bad thing, but I assure you, it was one of the most painful things that I ever had to endure. I remember the nurses coming in with the buckets and bandages. As soon as they come

KANISHA ANTHONY

in, I would quickly turn and pretend to be asleep, just to see if it would make them go and come back later, but it never worked. "Honey it's time to change your bandages," they would say. There was always about four nurses, because there were quite a lot of bandages to be changed. Along with the nurses, always came in an elderly lady with white hair that was sweet as pie, she was my moral support.

As the nurses would all stand there pouring water on the bandages and peeling them from my raw burnt skin, the elderly lady would stand by my side, holding my hand and telling me that everything will be okay.

"Squeeze my hand as hard as you want to," she would tell me as tears rolled down my face.

I would do just that and for some reason, it always seemed to make the pain a little more tolerable. The woman, whose name was Katie, would come to my room almost every day; I thought she was staff or the support staff at the hospital. I later came to find out, Katie was a volunteer who took time out to come see a little girl, and help her keep her mind off of the scary pains she had to go through every single day. They called her a volunteer, but I saw her as an angel. The sight of the nurses and their big bandages scared me, but each time that inevitable threat came along, I looked forward to seeing that angel who made the stormy waters in my heart still. Katie was always there every other day, and just like she always assured me, by the mere sight of her, I knew that even through the pains and trauma I was going through, everything was going to be okay.

She's not with us any longer today, but if she was I would want nothing but a big hug and to hear that voice again say, "everything will be okay."

During all the time I spent at Mercy Hospital St. Louis Missouri, I can remember some pretty amazing events that took place. When you think of a hospital, the normal things you'll imagine are sadness, hurt, and pain. But for the most part, I have thoughts of smiles, laughter, and love. Whenever I reminisce on those days, I remember the time my brother and I rode down the hallways, waving to patients and family members. I remember the times when I met other kids in the burn unit, some of whom had very sad stories.

For instance, there was a little girl in the room next to mine, who also had burn injuries. Her story was that she was put in a bathtub full of boiling water because her stepdad was upset with her mother. I didn't really understand back then, but what I do remember is that the little girl and 1 became friends in that hospital. We did crafts together, read books together and rode ponies together. (Yes they brought ponies to the hospital for kids to enjoy. That's awesome right?)

Even at Christmas, "Santa" came to visit and my room was full of gifts, stuffed animals, and cards from complete strangers. Talk about making a girl feel good on a Christmas when she couldn't go home. Although I wished I was home, I really enjoyed all the care and attention I was getting both from family members and from people who did not know me but were reaching out to me to strengthen me and put a smile on my face.

The healing process was a long process. I no longer knew how to do the things that I used to do. The half of my body that wasn't burned was almost in as much as pain as the other side of my body which was burned. To resuscitate my skin, and help the regeneration process, I had to go through what is called skin grafts. If you're not familiar with what a skin graft is, I'll break it down for you.

A skin graft is a medical procedure where a portion of your healthy skin is taken from a part of your body that is called the donor site and transplanted into a damaged part of the body, which is called a recipient site. The donor site is usually a part of your body that is covered by clothes- so that any scar on it won't be visible- but for me, it was every part of my body that wasn't burned, including my legs my stomach and my buttocks. During the procedure, the doctors would take two layers of your top skin and put it the area where it needs to be transplanted. Then they would dress it properly, for the donor skin to lap very well into the recipient site. After the skin graft surgery, they would wrap bandages around the wounded area, and every day the bandages would have to be taken off. The painful part of this procedure is that the bandages normally stick to the wounded skin, and when they peel it off, it drags the skin along. The pain is out of this world! Because of this, the nurses would always use cool water and soap to soften and get them off, after which they would put ointment on it. This painful procedure goes on every single day.

I had to heal from a lot of things before I could start doing the everyday normal activities again. I had to learn how to walk again and I also had to learn how to write again. When I was born I was born left-handed, but in the fire, three fingers on my left hand were burnt off, so on my left hand, I only have my thumb and my pinky. On my right hand, I only lost one finger, which was my pointer finger. At one point the doctor asked if we would like them to replace my fingers with my toes, but my family didn't agree to that.

Learning to do all of these things all over again was hard and frustrating. There were many times I just wanted to give up, but I didn't and in time I was able to go home.

Recovery is hard. One of the biggest obstacles to recovering is when you can't see yourself making any progress. It sometimes takes days, weeks, months, or even years; and at most points, you may feel like you're getting nowhere. It reaches the point where you want to give up. I am here to tell you that you are not alone. I am here to tell you that it is going to be okay.

Going through a life-changing experience can have a huge impact on one's life, as well as on their families. If you have ever come close to your life ending, or you have watched someone you loved dearly lose their life, you will understand that death and near-death experiences are the most frightening things anyone could ever go through.

I could not imagine what my mother had to go through after losing two children, having one in the hospital, and another that had to witness the whole thing. Just the thought of it brings me to tears.

My mom's road to recovery was much different from mine. Although I suffered from outer scars, she suffered from inner scars which I believe can be much worse than the outer.

It may be easy to say that I would have held myself together and bear it like one of the many challenges of life, but it is easier said than done. Truth is I don't know how I would have reacted. Maybe I would have risen above the whole challenge or maybe I would have turned to drugs to take the pain away. We all experience pain in life; some emotional, some physical, and we all handle them in different ways.

My mother lost her children.

My Grandmother lost her grandchildren.

My brother lost the only brothers he had.

My uncle lost his best friend.

And I can only imagine what was going through the minds of everyone else. My father, my grandparents, cousins, etc.

While I was in physical pain the rest of my family was in some serious emotional pain.

No pain is alike. And we must all walk the journey and path that God has for our lives. God made us to understand that there is a purpose for every pain. Jeremiah 29:11 says, "for I know the plans I have for you declares the lord" plans to prosper you and not harm you, plans to give you hope and future". You can go on each day knowing that God loves you and hears your cry.

Keep pushing forward no matter what happens and remember that pain is normal.

It's going to be hard, but you can and will get through it if you believe in God and in the grace, He has given you to surpass all your challenges.

CHAPTER 3

DEALING WITH THE STIGMA

As soon as I got home from the hospital, the first thing I did was to look in the mirror. I still couldn't understand why my hair was gone. Even with all the scars, to me, my hair mattered the most. I loved my hair so much, and I couldn't imagine living another day without it.

"Grandma" I would say running from the bathroom, "when is my hair coming back?" "I'm not sure," she responded." To me, "not sure" meant maybe tomorrow or the next day. So, every day I would go back into the bathroom and stare in the mirror to check if my hair was growing back. Day after day, I still couldn't see any trace of hair except for one small section on the right side of my head. This was the only section of my head that didn't get burned in the fire. The small section of hair would get washed, conditioned, and braided in one long braid just like it would be if I had a head full of hair. At home, I would walk around the house just like that, with my one braid hanging on the side of my face.

I was very conscious of it; I always prayed to wake up one day and see my head full of hair again, but after a while, I didn't mind it. I got used to not having hair, it seemed as if the rest of the family did too. To my family, I was still the same Kanisha I was before the incident happened. There were times I thought I would get special treatment, one time I was acting out and told my grandma "you can't spank me I have burns all over my body." Little did I know that nothing had changed, and she proved this to me one day when she found the one part of my body that had no scars and used what we called the "spank spank" stick, also known as the little rubber spatula to spank me. Till this day, I still appreciate her for that. I know it may seem strange to appreciate a spanking but I appreciate that she didn't make me feel different. I was just like anyone else even if that meant getting in trouble.

At the beginning, I stayed indoors most

of the time, and stayed out of the sight of the public. The few times I went out in those days, people stared a lot. Let's just say I wasn't your average little girl walking around the grocery store. I had to wear pressure garments called *jobst*. If you have never heard of these, then consider yourself lucky. It is an elastic bodysuit worn as a second skin to keep scars from forming (imagine having to wear one of those wets suits people use to scuba dive in). They had to be worn on every part of my body that had burns. This meant that I had to be covered from head to toe. First, there was the pants and then a shirt type vest that had to be zipped up in the back. Then there were the gloves, and last but not least, the face mask. It was very tight, very hot, and not fashionable at all. As I walked through the stores everyone would notice the little girl with the brown suit in the clear mask. There were days that I liked wearing them; sometimes it felt better that people were staring at the garments and not the burns. It did not matter because either way, they were staring. Being stared at wasn't fun at all. There were times when people stared and I would wonder what they were thinking. Their eyes made me feel different; they made me feel weird.

In my imaginations, I could hear them saying, "She's so ugly." "What is wrong with her?" "Gross." "Why do they even allow her to come out in public?" "What a freak."

Maybe they weren't really thinking in such directions, but the way they were looking at me made me feel like it. The looks on their faces almost drove me towards depression. They made me hate my existence and wish that I could just disappear. There were days when I just wanted to be like a turtle, crawl into my shell and never come out again. My family members would oftentimes get more upset than I did. They did not like to see the way people made faces and stared as if I was an alien. There were many times that I had to calm them down and tell them that it was okay. I didn't want them to get upset so I smiled and pretended like it didn't faze me in anyway. But of course, it did, I didn't like to feel different and I didn't understand why people had to be so cruel. I think one of the cruelest moments I ever had to go through in the public was one day when my Dad decided to take me and my siblings to an amusement park. I was so excited about that day and I decided to be brave and wear shorts. As we stood in line for what seemed to be hours, waiting to check in, I was laughing and giggling with my family, and then a woman walked up to us. She tapped my father's shoulder and asked, "Excuse me sir, but does your daughter have a disease? I don't want my kids standing that close in case they catch something." Talk about a stab in the heart! Her words cut so much deeper than a knife. I was so hurt that I no longer wanted to stand in that line. And although my family gave her a piece of their mind so much that she decided to leave, I just wanted to curl up in a ball and lay in my bed. I wasn't sure of how much more of the embarrassment and stigmatization I would be able to take; I just wished I could disappear from the surface of the earth and never come back.

Having people stare at you can be frustrating and very uncomfortable. Here is what I have learned over the years about people staring.

It is natural for people to stare when they see something different or out of the ordinary. It's really hard, but I've learned to try not to take it personally. I actually catch myself staring at others sometimes, not because I am judging that person, but because something about the person has caught my eye and made me so curious that I just couldn't get my eyes off. These things happen spontaneously without me thinking anything bad about the person.

One thing you must remember is that, while you are not in control of the staring. You are in control of how the staring affects you. The next time someone stares at you, you can choose to let it bother you or you can choose to brush it off.

One of my favorite things I do when people stare at me, especially when I walk into a room and everyone stares at once, I pretend like I'm a celebrity. Do you think Beyoncé gets offended when people stare at her? No way. She walks in the room fiercely like she owns the place.

If you ever happen to run into someone who looks different from you or any other person, and you get tempted to stare at them until they wish they could disappear, always remember that person you are staring at is a human being like you. It could have taken all they had to be brave enough and step out in public that day. Remember that it can be very uncomfortable for them, and if you catch yourself staring and they happen to catch you, smile. Smiling is so contagious.

If you are a parent, and you have a child that is pointing and staring, it's ok. Don't feel embarrassed, they are children, and as I stated before, they see something they don't see every day. As a parent, I encourage you to talk to your children at home about differences. Explain to them that all people look different. Find books that will help them understand. Teach them that how we treat each other is far more important than how someone looks. I always tell the kiddos that if they see someone who looks different from them, smile, and say hi, then later they can ask questions privately, so that they don't hurt that person's feelings.

One of my favorite quotes by Fred Rogers says *"As different as we are from one another, as unique as each one of us is, we are more the same than we are different."* That may be the most essential message of all, as we help our children grow toward being caring, compassionate and charitable adults."

CHAPTER 4

SCHOOL/BULLYING

For me, home meant solace. It meant defense, it was a safe haven where everyone protected me from the cruelty of the world around me, but there was no way I could stay under that protection forever. I feared that someday, something was definitely going to come and puncture that umbrella that shielded me from the rains of human cruelty, and just as I feared, school came along and turned my daydreams into nightmares.

It was my first day in school; I was standing in line outside on the sidewalk anticipating one of the biggest days of my life. Like any other kid, I was nervous, with lots of butterflies flying around inside my belly. This won't be too bad, I thought to myself and as I climbed the black stairs of that big yellow school bus. As I looked back, waved at my mom, and she snapped pictures, my heart dropped, all of a sudden I felt uncomfortable. That safe place that I had was finally gone now. My people that had once been my protectors we're no longer there by my side. It was as if I was in a world that I knew nothing about. After searching for an empty seat, I became so jittery that I suddenly sat in the first empty seat I seen.

"What happened to you?" a voice next to me asked." "I was in a fire," I said softly. "Well, where are your fingers?" the voice asked again.

"They got burned off in the fire," I said again, hoping that would be the last question.

"Well, where is your hair," the boy asked once more.

"it was burned off too" I responded.

"Well, you look like a freak and I don't want you to sit by me."

At that moment I stood up with tears in my eyes and moved to the next seat.

"Sit down" the bus driver yelled, and so I did. This time I sat next to a little girl that didn't have any words for me but made sure she pushed herself all the way to the window, so that I was not able to touch her.

Throughout the rest of the ride to the school, I buried my head down into my book bag, wishing that I could somehow turn invisible. Obviously, that didn't happen, and finally we had arrived at the school. As I walked down from the bus everyone made sure to move out of the way so that the burned girl wouldn't touch them.

I was relieved once I made it into a classroom. The thought of an adult being in the room made me feel safe. There was no way she would let the kids say bad things about me. I soon found the desk with my name on it, set down and put my hands together to see my fingers. Soon, the teacher stood in front of the class; "What's your name," she asked looking directly at me.

"Me? Oh, my name is Kanisha" I responded.

"Kanisha will you please take off your hat in the classroom we have a no hat policy"

"My mother talked to the school and they said that I can wear my hat," I replied.

"I was not told anything about that, so please take your hat off"

As my eyes filled with tears, the second time within an hour, I slowly pulled back the bonnet looking hat and sat it on my desk.

The whole class stared at the bald, lumpy, discolored head with the one braid hanging over the right ear.

"Honey, I am so sorry I didn't know.

You can put your hat back on," the teacher said apologetically.

From that moment onwards, I knew I wouldn't like this thing called school. I went home that day and walked in the door with a huge smile.

"How was school?" they asked me.

"It was great; I had so much fun" I replied, still feigning the huge smile on my face.

That was my thing; I knew that when I got hurt, my family hurt even more, so I always tried my best to hold it in. I didn't let them know that I was hurting so bad inside and that honestly, I never wanted to go to school again.

After spending a year in kindergarten at this particular school it was time to move. At the end of kindergarten, I finally began to wear wigs. At first, it was a little different because I wasn't used to it, but eventually I started to love them. The fact that I was able to have hair on my head was astonishing to me and for the most part, no one knew about it. I could take them off at night and put them on the next day and be ready for school. Looking at the pictures now, they weren't the most attractive wigs in the world, but they worked. They helped my self-esteem so much and did a lot to change the way I felt about myself and the way others seen me.

I entered into my new school feeling different from the way I felt before. I had a good dose of self-esteem and confidence working for me. I was so happy and optimistic that my new-found bravery was going to help me weather whatever storm that was possibly coming my way. Even though I still had all of my scars, there was something about the wigs that made me feel like the scars were not even there. Remember how badly I wanted my hair to grow back? I felt like it finally did, and that alone was a reason to be joyful!

Of course, other people notice the scars, but for a brief time, I felt normal again. I was the first person in the class and as I sat at my first-grade desk, my teacher politely walked up to me and said that if I had any problems, I should come directly to her and she would handle it. "Wow," I thought, "this year is going to be awesome!" It was just the first day, and it was already so different from my last school.

As the students started walking in, I recognized someone. "Oh no, it's the same boy that was at my other school." He was so mean to me and used to pick on me every chance he got. Maybe this time, things will be different, I hoped, and gave him the benefit of doubt that maybe he changed during the summer. And as he kept walking he stopped at the desk right behind me. I slowly turned around, smiled and said hi very nervously. Quite to my surprise, he replied with a "hi." Maybe he didn't recognize me I thought, and as the first hour of class went by, I felt at peace again.

Soon it was time for lunch. The teacher rounded up the class and grabbed her stuff to go for her lunch break, and almost immediately, it happened. The horror, the pain, the embarrassment started.

The little boy behind me that I had just thought changed, hadn't changed one bit. As a matter of fact, he was worse. I wondered how I could have thought that someone like that could ever change. All the while, I was in the class and fantasizing about how this school year was going to be awesome because there would be no bullies, little did I know that the kid behind me, who just replied to my greetings like a sensible person, was busy in his mind planning on how to humiliate me.

He was just waiting for his chance and as the teacher turned around; he reached out, grabbed my wig from my head and threw it on the floor. A burst of laughter roared across the classroom, as I fell out of my seat on the floor in a fetal position to cover my head and put my wig on at the same time. You're probably thinking, "Wow! How could a kid act like this, how could a kid be so cruel?" I wondered the same thing many times.

Although I had a wonderful teacher who tried really hard to protect me, the kids still found a way to bully me. At recess, they would play tag and whoever won had to chase me, pull off my wig and make it to the top of the monkey bars. This went on for a while, all the way into the second grade. That was until my brother started going to school with me. My brother was somewhat my hero; anytime he heard of someone picking on me, he would be right there to teach them a lesson. It was nice for a while until he started getting in so much trouble, that he was suspended from school a lot.

Bullying is real and it can happen anywhere and to anybody. We have all heard the saying *"sticks and stones can break my bones, but words can never hurt me"* at least once in our lives. I grew up hearing that from a lot of people, I believed it. I thought that I was weak for letting words hurt me, but here is the thing: as an adult, I have learned that words absolutely do hurt. Words can leave scars internally just as easy as you can get a scar on the outside.

Unfortunately, there will be people in your life that will have absolutely nothing nice to say. What is even more unfortunate is that you start hearing these words as a child. Too often, kids that are bullied try to suck it up, they hide it from family and from teachers. This comes from feeling embarrassed or ashamed. For me, I felt all that and more. But being silent seemed to make things worse. Coming home from school, I smiled and pretended like everything was ok, but it wasn't. It felt horrible.

How was anyone supposed to know that? How was anyone supposed

to help me?

It may seem terrifying to ask for help, but it will make you feel less afraid. If you are in school, find a trusted adult and let them know what is happening. If they do nothing to help you, find someone else. Maybe it could be a parent, a teacher, a guidance counselor, a coach, or a pastor.

Hoping the bully will go away will not make it go away, but standing up to it, challenging it upfront and developing an inner shock-absorber will help you get through it.

As an adult you play a big role in helping to prevent bullying. Parents, there are many resources that can help. Start off by trying to recognize any warning signs your child may have if involved in bullying. They may not always be the one being bullied, they could be bullying others or witnessing the bullying.

Warning signs a child is being bullied

- Feeling helpless or lack of self esteem
- Unexplained injuries
- Lost or destroyed items such as

clothing, books, electronics

- Frequent headaches or stomach aches, feeling sick or faking illness
- Changes in eating habits, like suddenly skipping meals or binge eating. Kids may come home from school hungry because they didn't eat at school
- Difficulty sleeping or frequent nightmares
- Sudden loss of friends or avoidance of social situations
- Declining grades, loss of interest in schoolwork or not wanting to go to school
- Self-destructive behaviors such as rung away from home, harming themselves, or talking about suicide

Warning signs a child is bullying others

- Get into physical or verbal fights
- Have friends who bully others
- Blame others for their problems
- Are increasingly aggressive
- Get sent to the principal's office or detention frequently
- Have unexplained extra money or new belongings
- Don't accept responsibility for their actions
- Are competitive and worry about their reputation or popularity

Baby Kanisha in 1989

Photo of my mom brothers and I before the fire

From left to right Marquis age 3 (survivor) Mom(survivor) Marcus age 1(deceased) Travis age 6 (deceased) Kanisha age 4 (survivor)

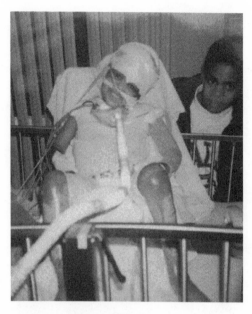

Kanisha in the hospital bandaged up, connected to a feeding tube (still smiling) with uncle DeShawn by her side.

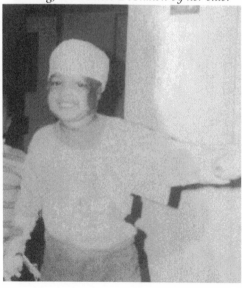

Kanisha walking the hallways of the hospital in arm cast.

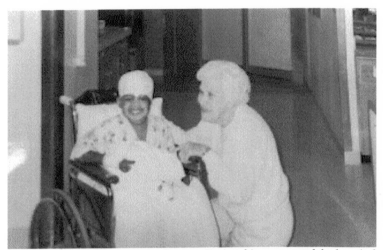

Kanisha and sweet support volunteer Katie taking a tour of the hospital

Pony rides at Ranken Jordan Hospital

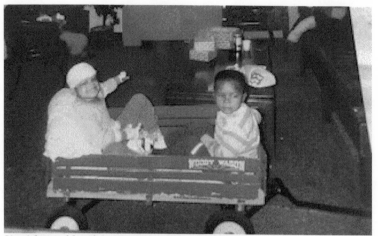

Kanisha and brother Marquis visiting patients around the hospital

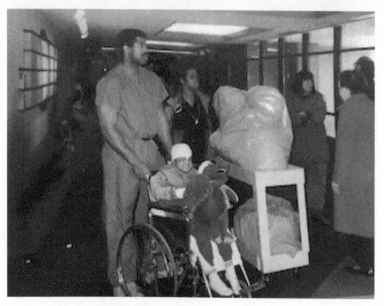

Kanisha finally heading home.

Kanisha and Marquis pictured with officer Keith Cummins and Sgt. Harry Belcher at award ceremony.

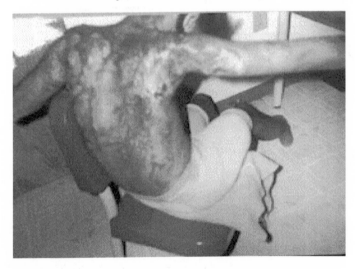

Kanisha's scarred back and a glimpse of pressure garments

Kanisha pictured wit her dad at award ceremony

Rare photo of Kanisha with both parents

Kanisha, Uncle (Deshawn) and Brother (Marquis) pose for picture

Kanisha on the First day of school

Photo of Kanisha's missing fingers on both hands

Calvin and Kanisha on one of their first dates

77

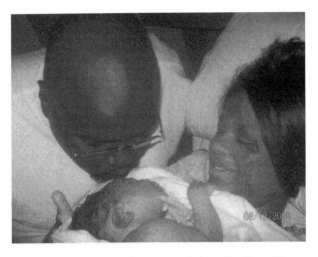

Photo of Calvin and Kanisha and their first born Trey

Calvin and Kanisha's wedding day

Kanisha welcomes Daughter Mariah into the world

Kanisha with son and daughter honoring the fire department on her birthday

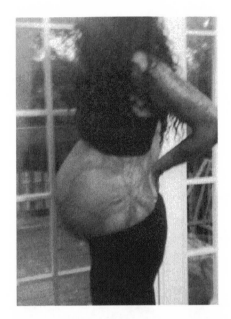

Bare belly photo of kanisha's pregancy

Kanisha and family on delivery day of her son Kristopher

Calvin and Kanisha visiting the camp where they met with their children

Before and after of Kanisha without wig

Kanisha and family 2018

CHAPTER 5

WHO AM I?

Amongst everything I suffered as a result of the fire, one of the most gruesome things I had to live with was a lack of identity. The fire did not only take away my pretty face, my beautiful body, fingers and my long hair; it also took away my identity. Everyone else had a name attached to them, which was the way they were identified, but my case was different. It was as if my name, Kanisha, was just a fantasy, which only appeared on paper.

For the most part, Kanisha stopped defining me; the fire, its burns and scars took over.

"Who am I?" I remember asking myself this question over and over again. Most days, I would sit on the bathroom sink staring at myself in the mirror, and wondering who I am. I would say the words, "Who am I?" slowly and tentatively, with a part of me genuinely waiting for the girl in the mirror to give me an answer to this question that bugged my mind. It was as if I was staring at a stranger. Had I lost myself? You see I have been called many things after the fire; so many things that it was as if I no longer knew what my real identity was. When people talked about me they would always describe the physical parts of me. I was no longer Kanisha; I was now the burnt girl. I was now the scarred one. I don't believe many people meant any harm when they said these things it was as if it was in the nature of humans to describe each other by the way they looked.

I was in sixth grade, and just like any other day, I was sitting in my seat at the back of the classroom as far away as possible from anyone else when I heard, "Beep" can you please have Kanisha come down to the office." It was the voice of the secretary speaking loudly over the intercom.

My first thought was I really don't want to get up in front of everyone and walk out of the room. Second thought was why in the world am I being called down to the office?

I gathered my stuff and slowly made my way to the door. Hoping someone else would distract the class so all eyes wouldn't be on me. Once I got to the office one of my favorite ladies in the school greeted me. It was my counselor and I simply admired her. She always made me feel like I was somebody. Well, until that day.

"Hi, honey," she greeted, "you're not in trouble. Please have a seat and I will let the principal know you're here." She then popped her head into the principal's office. "Which student is here to see me the principal asked?"

"The girl with the scars," she quietly whispered.

The lady that had once made me feel like I was on top of the world made me to feel like a nobody that day.

I walked into the principal's office

trying my best not to shed a tear. I was not in trouble at all; in fact, I was being given an award, that to this day I can't remember what it was about because as the principal was talking, all I could hear was "the girl with the scars" repeating over and over in my head.

I was tired of being identified with the burns and scars. I wanted nothing more, but for people to call me by my name. And after that day I was determined to make it happen.

For the rest of that year, I made it a point to correct anyone who called me anything other than my name. I had scars, but I was not my scars. I was tired of being the victim. I was tired of crying and I was tired of hiding. And with that attitude, I developed just the amount of confidence that I needed.

I began to walk around school with my head held high. No longer was I looking down at the ground when someone looked at me. I held my shoulders high, my head up, and kept a smile on my face always. Evidently, it started to work, because people were starting to treat me different. They weren't staring at me, they weren't laughing anymore and they were starting to treat me like a human being. As a matter of fact, the popular girls asked me to sit at their table by the end of the year. To me, this was the highlight of the year. Going from being the least liked girl in school to hanging out with the coolest girls in school- yeah that was big. That summer, we all hung out a lot. We went to the movies, we went to the mall and I even got invited to my first sleepover. We spent the night talking about boys, eating snacks, and tee-peeing the neighbor's house. It was something like out of a movie for me. Staying at this huge house having the time of my life with friends was something I never expected to happen for me. The next morning, we were woken up to go clean up the mess we made at the neighbor's house followed by a girl's day out of skating. We finished cleaning and rushed to take our showers and to get dressed. I was one of the first to finish getting ready I covered my body with Vaseline and sat down to wait for the rest of the girls. At one point I had walked downstairs to grab something as I was walking back up I overheard them talking about a grease stain that was left on the chair that I was sitting in. "Eww... how much grease does she need?" one of the girls asked. As I walked in the room everyone became quiet. The rest of that day was miserable. Out of every other day, *Aunt Flo* decided to come to town. "Are you serious? I thought to myself; the first day of ever having a period, had to be today? I sat on the bench in the skating rink, feeling embarrassed and waiting for one of the moms to bring me a jacket to cover up the blood. I had to leave early so I could go home and change. No one wanted to talk to me. No one wanted to sit by me. And every time I looked around they were whispering and staring at me. I went home that night and didn't let anyone know that I started the big "p" word.

The rest of the summer I never heard from the girls. I called, got driven to their houses and even made and bought them stuff so they would start talking to me again. I know it was a pathetic thing to do, but I wanted so deeply for someone to like me.

When the new school year began I braved up and wore a skirt to school for the first time. My grandmother reminded me before I left the house, to put enough Vaseline on my skin so that it wouldn't get dry. So, I did.

I got to the school, walked into my classroom, and found my seat. Next thing I know, a boy walled by and knocked all of my books off my desk. I bend over to pick them up and once again burst of laughter goes across the room. "GREESEBALL" screamed a group of girls from the back. I turn around and there they were the girls that I spent the summer with. It was so heartbreaking to see the girls who I thought were my friends pointing and laughing at me.

Do what others say about you bother you? Of course, it does at least for most of us. Maybe you have been called the Fat girl or the skinny girl in the room. Or in my case, you have scars and are identified by that. Or maybe it isn't so much of your outer appearance maybe people say you are too loud, too quiet, lazy, etc. Whatever it is, it's something we all have gone through in life. And at some point, we have stopped and actually believed it.

And somewhere in between being called that and believing it-even for a brief second-we got stuck and somehow let that become our identity. We do this because we look for our self-worth by seeking it from others. All of a sudden, we wake up one day and it becomes very important how others view us. It could be by what we are wearing, our physical appearance, what kind of car we drive, or even how much money we make. And as a result, we look for reassurance and praise from our peers to feel okay about ourselves.

Here's the thing: it is not what others think about us that matters; it's our emotional well-being that depends on how we feel about ourselves.

I once read an article by psychotherapist Anne-Marie Alger that *"Our sense of self – our 'identity' – should not come from what others think about us, how we look, or how we behave."* Many of us have heard these and many wise sayings all through our lives, yet we worry about being judged or measured by others and falling short of their requirements.

And because of this, we put on an act, a facade, a mask, and try to be who we are not, just because we want to "belong." We all do it at times – present the 'best-self' out there, when inside, we may be feeling very different from the real 'me' hiding underneath- but when this becomes a norm, it could be a problem.

Such dependency on external validation prevents the real 'you' from being out there, and impacts on personal growth, as well as the opportunity for happiness. Low self-esteem can be linked to issues from the past, from childhood and parental neglect, from abuse and trauma, from childhood bullying, and this often shapes how we view ourselves and then how we interact with others. These feelings can be re-triggered by major life events or a change in life circumstances. There can be a longing for social acceptance and reassurance from others; to be noticed, to be loved, to be wanted and needed, to be cared about. If you have low self-esteem, you may not like yourself very much,

and there is a tendency to seek your self-worth from external sources and relationships that become increasingly important and sometimes unhealthy, in order to make us happy.

When I started hanging with those girls I wasn't being myself. I started to act any kind of way I thought they would accept me as. I began talking like them, dressing like them and doing things they told me to just so I could feel like I belonged. And this wasn't the only time; I did this well into adulthood. I became very good at pretending like I fit in. I did things I didn't actually enjoy doing, went places I didn't want to go and talked about things I could care less about. In return, I lost myself even more along with the so-called "friends" I was hanging with.

In the past few years, this is what I have learned; you don't have to do anything for someone to become your friend or for you to find value in yourself. Don't ever feel like you must do certain things or give your identity up for them to value you. You are enough being you.

Psalm 139:13-15Amplified Bible (AMP)

13

For You formed my innermost parts;

You knit me [together] in my mother's womb.
14

I will give thanks and praise to You, for I am
fearfully and wonderfully made;
Wonderful are Your works,
And my soul knows it very well.
15

My frame was not hidden from You,
When I was being formed in secret,
And intricately and skillfully formed [as if
embroidered with many colors] in the depths
of the earth.

Yes, we all have flaws of some sort and at some point, in your life; people will use them against you. But once you start to embrace them and accept yourself as you are, which is the first step towards finding your identity, you will begin to love yourself more and more every day.

Look at your flaws as unique traits of yourself. Those flaws are the things that make you different from the seven billion other people in the world. Take them, embrace them and use them to your advantage. They have a purpose. You have a purpose. Never forget that.

CHAPTER 6

AN UNEXPECTED TURN OF LIFE

Have you ever wished you could disappear from the face of the earth? Have you ever wished you could close your eyes and make all your pains and frustrations go away?

Well, that is the way I felt in Middle School. I didn't want to be around the people that were in that school any longer. I wanted to run away from all my problems. I wanted to move to a whole new state, and that was exactly what happened.

My mother and her boyfriend moved to the state of Delaware a year before I started 6th grade. At this point, I was living with my grandmother, and visiting my father every other weekend. Since my parents were separated, there were certain rules we had to go by. One of the rules was that I wasn't allowed to leave the state without the other parent's or the court's permission.

Well, one day my mother decided to break those rules. She came to visit and told us that this time we could come visit her. So, we did just that; my brother and I hopped in the car with our suitcases and traveled on the road for what felt like days. Eventually, we made it to the small state of Delaware, and my mom dropped news that made it seem like all my dreams had just come true. She announced that we were not visiting them; we were actually moving there.

{After the fire happened mom wasn't herself anymore. She was hurting. She was in pain from losing her two kids and watching her other two go through life changing situations. She had turned to drugs and alcohol to try to numb the pain she was going through, all while having a mental break down.}

When we arrived to our new apartment everything was all set up, we had our own rooms and my mom seemed like she had really gotten herself together.

I was so elated, I no longer had to be

with those mean and cruel kids at my school. This was the beginning of a new Journey, and this time I was sure that it would be different.

School started and it wasn't bad, of course people still stared; after all, the scars were still there. Not too many people said anything wrong, I was the new girl. I was going to make sure that I made a great impression, even if I had to tell a few white lies. For example, I told everyone that I was from St. Louis, and that Nelly was my cousin and we had dinner together every weekend as a family, actually I was from a town about 30 minutes away from St. Louis and I had never even been to a Nelly concert before. Everyone said that I had an accent so, of course, I purposely flaunted it at times. In all, people were really nice and I made friends very fast.

Basically, all my problems were solved, at least they seemed to be.

After a couple of weeks of living with in Deleware, things began to change. My mother's boyfriend started to lose his temper often. It would all start from a flare of anger, then the anger would turn into yelling, and the yelling would turn into physical violence.

This was not the first time that I was seeing my mother being abused, but this time, it was different. The other times, I was only a little girl, but now I was older and I could understand things more than I used to, so I always felt every bit of her pains. Every punch, every slap, every hit, and every scream got to me. I felt them all in my heart. There were times where I wanted to trade places with her and take the pain away from her. I wanted to defend her from the person that was abusing her, and then run away with her and my brother in the middle of the night, but it never happened. I know that she wouldn't have even paid any mind to me if I suggested that we run away, because after the abuse at night, by morning everything was always back to normal, and they would be all over each other like they were an inseparable pair.

Maybe he will stop, I said to myself, but he didn't. Sometimes it took weeks, and sometimes it just took a few days for the cycle to repeat itself again.

If physically abusing my mother was his only flaw, maybe it would have been tolerable; pending the time that my mom would come to terms with reality and decide to walk away from him. That was not it, sometimes, he drank himself to stupor, but worse of all, he was a pervert.

There I was, sitting in the dark at about 3:00 a.m.; I was staring out the window, knowing that it would only be a matter of time before my door would creak open. "One, two, three, four, five, six, seven," I would start counting in my head, finally I heard the door open. "Close your eyes, close your legs, roll into a ball, and pretend like you're asleep, and maybe, just maybe he will go away," I tried convincing myself. Who was I kidding? He did not care, he had been drinking and just had got done beating my mom just a few hours before. He had absolutely no care in the world if I was sleep or not.

I wrapped myself in three blankets that night and wore extra layers, hoping that the longer it would take to get my clothes off, the longer I had time to come up with a plan.

It was too late; he was already on top of me. I wanted so badly to scream for my mom to come to my rescue. Or maybe even have the courage to grab the hammer that had been hiding under my pillows for months, hit him on the head, grab my mom and brother and escape.

It sounded like a heroic thing to do, but instead I laid there with tears flowing down my face, helpless.

Was this the plan God had for my life? Did he really plan for me to be an 11-year-old girl whose virginity was taken by her mom's boyfriend, who had to go through the terror of being raped repeatedly almost every night?

If it was so, then I wanted nothing to do with it. At this point, those girls laughing at me didn't sound bad at all.

This was a subject that I used to feel very uncomfortable talking about, It still chokes me up even as I'm writing this.

Sexual abuse is real, and it is a serious matter which has not yet gotten the attention it deserves. The reason why most of us do not want to talk about it is because we feel guilty. No matter how many times you have tried not to let the guilt shut you up, some way or the other, the guilt always seems to come back. You try to think of all the ways you could have stopped it from happening. Then you start thinking of all the ways it would bring shame to your family. If you are reading this now and you have been a victim of sexual abuse, I want you to know it is not and never will be be your fault. No matter how many times you have thought about how you could have avoided the situation, the offender is always the one at fault.

If you have ever been a victim of sexual abuse, you may have certain feelings such as depression, shame, fear, anxiety, flashbacks, lack of self-confidence or anger to name a few. One of the biggest things I felt and still feel as a survivor of sexual abuse is shame and embarrassment. I never wanted to talk to anyone about it because, well, I just felt dirty. My silence never helped me, I just bottled up a lot of negative emotions, put on a cape and kept moving, while I was dying slowly inside.

Honestly, I thought that not talking about it would make me forget about it, which would eventually make me heal, but that was far from the truth. From time to time, it always came back fresh in my mind like it happened just last night. Sometimes, I would see certain things or hear certain noises that would give me flashbacks and nightmares for days.

I eventually started opening up about it to a few people who were close to me. Although I opened up, the problem was that I opened up to the wrong people. They made it seem like what happened to me, wasn't a big deal. I've heard things like "that was a long time ago, you should be over it by now," or "It happens to a lot of girls, my friend went through it, you'll be fine."

Let me say this, It doesn't matter how long ago it happened to you. There is a grief in sexual assault that you can't just "get over." At some point, you will grow and start healing, but there will always be that feeling of grief.

People will tell you that it happens to a lot of girls, just like they told me; but I want you to know that no matter how many times it may have happened to someone else, that doesn't make it right, and it doesn't make your experience a minor one either, even if it sounds like others had worse experiences. You endured that pain, you suffered the loss of your innocence. Do not let anyone make you feel like its "fine." It is not, and you're allowed to grieve about it.

I also have had the question "did you fight back?" "It couldn't have been that bad if you didn't fight back." Shamefully I answered, "No I did not fight back, I froze." Each and every time I froze, I used to think that that was absolutely crazy of me to do that, but the fact is: it is very common for one to freeze. Studies have shown that your body shuts down in shock, making it difficult to move, speak or even think.

With all that being said, I encourage you to talk to someone about what you went through and endeavor to talk to the right person. It could be a friend or a close family member, but if you feel like one of them can't be trusted, then you have to reach out to someone else. You can see a therapist or call the rape crisis hotline.

Just because you don't talk about it doesn't mean that it didn't happen. More shame can come from hiding the truth. I know it is scary, but talking to someone will help set you free from the prison you feel like you are in.

CHAPTER 7

SEEKING LOVE AND FINDING PEACE

The rape and sexual abuse went on for a while and although I told my mother, she did nothing. To her defense, I honestly believe that she was doing it out of love. I hate to think that my mom placed her boyfriend ahead of me. That she cared more about how he would feel, than she cared about the pain I had to go through every other day. I choose to push that assertion into the darkest part of my heart, so I've made myself to believe she was too scared to do something. My mom was scared of what would happen if she did anything about it, so she decided to do nothing at all because in her head that was the safest option. With that being said, I have no hatred in my heart for my mother. I love her with every bit of my heart. And have grown to understand the power of forgiveness. (we will talk more on forgiveness in a few pages.)

I spent less than a year in Delaware. Remember earlier when I told you I wasn't allowed out of the state without Court approval? Well, that caught up with us, the whole time I was gone, my dad was trying to figure out how to get me back. Eventually, he did, the day he arrived, my mom found out that he was in town and had me hide over at a friend's house. It wasn't that I didn't want to go with my Dad or that I didn't want to get away; It was just that I didn't want to leave my mom and brother alone. Obviously, you don't always get what you want in life, so the next day, I took that what-felt-like-several-days' journey back to Missouri. I knew that going back to Missouri was going to change so many things, and bring back some memories that I thought I had left behind.

My dad lived a good life. He and my mother weren't together after my birth, but he had always been a part of my life. He had his wife, their four children (my 3 brothers and 1 sister), a big house in the suburbs and a nice job. He welcomed me with open arms. I finished off middle school, started high school and he even sent me to have more surgeries for my Burns.

I found good friends, I had nice clothes, I lived in a beautiful home, and I had what many people would call the life.

I smiled every day, but really, I was back to not knowing who I was.

In High School, I start getting into boys a lot more, but boys didn't seem like they were that into me. I was too shy to actually talk to them. I had gorgeous friends that had boyfriends that I could only dream to have someday. One day I had the courage to call my crush. We talked on the phone all weekend, only for him to come to school on Monday and tell everyone all the embarrassing things I said to him on the phone. He stopped me in the hall with his group of boys and said, "You think I would ever do anything with you?" He and his boys walked off laughing and making fun of me with the sexual innuendos I said to him. I gave up the thought of having a boyfriend at that school; I didn't even have any crushes anymore. They were all just a joke to me.

Eventually I met a guy online, he was actually a friend of a friend, so that made me feel safe. We started talking on the phone daily, this went on for months, and just to avoid any surprises and embarrassments in the future, I explained to him that I was in a fire accident and had scars. We eventually met up in person, and he told me I was beautiful. One of the most beautiful girls he'd ever seen. I fell in love with him, I wanted him to meet my friends and family, and I wanted to meet his, but every time I asked, he was always too busy. Most of our relationship was just talking on the phone, at some point, he graduated from high school and moved to a new state.

When he moved I wanted to see him more than ever, and he convinced me to buy a plane ticket to come visit, I did just that. I saved up my money from the job I had and secretly went to a different state without my father's permission.

I nervously got off the plane, got a taxi and went to his house almost a thousand miles away from home.

He greeted me with a hug and said that we were going to have a fantastic weekend.

I knew that we would have sex, after all, that was all he always talked about. In my head, I had finally found someone that loved me, for me, and that was all I really wanted.

That night, I laid in his bed as he walked into the room. He bent over to whisper in my ear, and said, "I have something for you, don't be offended." Then he handed me a paper bag to put on my head, and gloves to wear so that it looked like I wasn't missing any fingers. The sad part was that I did it.

As we had intercourse that night, that paper bag covered my ugly face, but most of all, it covered the tears pouring down. As If I wasn't feeling worthless enough, that night proved to me that I had no kind of worth.

I felt so miserable, I told myself I wasn't pretty enough, that no man would ever love these scars. I told myself that I would be better off gone from this world. Yet, I continued to search for someone to love me. They all would tell me they loved me, and each time, I fell for it.

In my head, sex had become love. I didn't care about saving myself because I didn't see any reason to. A man had already taken my virginity when I was a little girl, so why even try to save myself now?

It got to a point where I just no longer cared. I started to sleep with guys just because that was my way of feeling like I was a human, like I was beautiful. Although it sounds crazy now, it all made sense to me back then.

After listening to people around me and also the voices in my head, I convinced myself that I was never going to get married, I didn't want to, it wasn't important. I could live my life without a man, because no man would ever love me.

The thought of having a child would make me sick to my stomach. I even refused to take child development class in high school, because there was no way I was ever having a child.

Doctors told me it was impossible, others told me no one would ever have a baby with me. You know what? I believed every word they said.

The reason why I said that every victim of sexual abuse or abuse of any kind should talk to someone is because I did not, and in return, that silence dealt a heavy blow on my self-esteem, and left me feeling worthless.

I felt like I had no worth at all; and what happens when you don't see worth of a thing? You begin to treat it very poorly.

Have you ever felt like this before? Have you ever felt like you had no significance or no purpose? If you have, you know how overwhelming these feelings can get.

So how do you make this feeling go away? How do you tackle it?

The first thing you need to do is to break the silence. Pray and ask God for peace and comfort. Pray for him to give you the grace to forgive yourself, although you didn't do anything wrong. Guilt can be overwhelming, and sometimes, it requires a special kind of grace for one to shake guilt off and move on with life. Also, ask God to bring the right people into your life to encourage you. You were not meant to do this alone. Don't pretend that you can handle it on your own. If you do, people will assume that you can, and they'll leave you to bear the burden all alone.

Secondly, remind yourself that you are not worthless. God created you and nothing that God created is of little or no worth. You are hand-made, custom-built, unique, and loved by God.

One thing that helped me overcome the feeling of worthlessness was that I decided to forgive myself. I felt so guilty about the things that I was doing with other men that even when I stopped, I still just had so much guilt building up inside me.

Let's talk about forgiveness for a bit:

When was the last time you have forgiven someone for something they did to you? When was the last time you stopped and actually forgave yourself?

Robert Enright wrote in his book **8 Keys to Forgiveness**, that *"the benefit of forgiveness is often more for the one who is hurt."*

I know that this may sound just a bit crazy, but it's true. When you don't forgive someone, you are holding on to bitterness and it'll cause you to start thinking badly of others.

Imagine every time someone did something to you, you had to carry around a 50-pound bag on your back. That 50-pound bag starts to hold you back; it's preventing you from moving forward. The day you choose to forgive is the day that you are able to take that bag off of your back.

Forgiveness allows you to simply be able to put the burden down. And just like that, you are free from it. It no longer belongs to you.

But imagine what would happen if you choose not to forgive. Imagine living for months or even years with that baggage, not to mention all the other baggage you collect along the way.

Laden with all that baggage, you will begin to start resenting others. And a lot of times you will transfer the aggression to others and start lashing out at people who had nothing to do with it. As if that's not enough, your heart will be filled with so much negative emotions that you won't have any space to see the beauty that life surrounds you with. If you are ever feeling like you are carrying too much baggage from unforgiveness; do yourself the favor to forgive so that you can be set free.

The day I chose to forgive the man who was coming into my room night after night, using me to please himself, putting me in pain just so he could feel pleasure, and taking away the one gift God had given me to one day give to the man I'll get married to, was the day I became free. The day I decided to forgive my mother for doing nothing when I confessed to her what her boyfriend had done to me, was the day I became free. The day I forgave the man that put a bag over my head while we were being intimate because he was so disgusted by the way I looked, was the day I became free. The day I decided to forgive all those people for picking on me, calling me ugly, pulling off my wig and teasing me for something I couldn't control, was the day I became free.

Imagine where my life would have been if I was never strong enough to forgive any of those things. I would have been like a walking corpse. It is one thing to have physical scars, and it is another thing to have scars inside the heart. You may not be in control of the scars you have on your body; you may not be the one to decide when they'll heal, but you are in total control of the scars inside your heart. Those scars will continue to hurt you;, the pain will continue to run deep, and your heart will continue to bleed until the day you get up and say, "It's enough! Scars, be gone!"

I decided to be in charge of my own happiness. I decided there was no way in the world I would let those people or circumstances control my life. Your happiness is in your own hands; don't you dare give it to anyone else.

Happiness is a decision; and just like every other decision, you have to be the one to make it yourself and to do it; you will have to understand that what people think, say or feel about you, does not matter. The only thing that matters is you!

I'm not saying that forgiveness is easy. It's not. I mean let's be for real, most of the time you are forgiving a person that is not even sorry. Those friends I forgave are not even sorry at all. Some of them have even forgotten that they hurt me. It didn't mean anything to them, so I was the only one suffering from the experience.

Remember though that when you forgive someone it doesn't mean you are accepting their behavior or that you are going to trust them again all of a sudden. It doesn't even mean that you should forget what happened. What it means is that you are simply deciding to let go of that guilt and anger that you have been holding on to. You're forgiving them for you. You're forgiving them so you can take hold of your life again. It takes a strong person to forgive, but I'm here to tell you that you have the strength to do so.

CHAPTER 8

WHEN LOVE HAPPENS

It was a Friday evening and as always, I sat in my room, isolated from the rest of my family. I loved my dad and my siblings and I was thankful that I had a place to live, but I never felt like I was one of them. So, I was taking every chance I got to be by myself.

That night I started to clean my room. I cleaned the room thoroughly for what seemed like hours. Eventually, I got tired and took a break. And as I sat on the floor in the middle of my room, I looked up and saw a piece of paper falling down to my lap. To this day I swear it came from the sky. But it may have also just been from my tall dresser where I kept all my papers; who knows?!

On that piece of paper, it was written, "Big Daddy" with a number on it.

When I was 10 years old I got a chance to experience one of the best weeks of my life. I was invited to a camp for burn survivors. And although I was nervous to go, when I got there, it felt like I was in a different world. Every single person at that camp looked just like me. Some were not as severe, while others were way more severe, but everyone had scars. This was a place where I no longer felt different. This was the place where I didn't feel like I had to pretend like I was someone else.

It was a week of friendship, challenges, singing, dancing, and laughing. I met some of the most amazing people. One of those people happened to be this guy everyone called "Big Daddy"

So with the paper in my hand, I picked up the phone and dialed the number. I later came to find out that his name wasn't actually big Daddy; it was Calvin and I'm sure his mom thought it was a little strange when I called and asked for him by that name.

Calvin and I talked on the phone for hours that night. It had been years since we had spoken and so we spent that time catching up on each other's lives.

Every single day after that, we didn't miss a day without talking to each other. And I mean every day. I would wake up to go to school and he was still on the phone snoring away. I even remember a few times where I got in trouble for having him on the phone in my pocket while sitting at the dinner table.

A couple of months later on Valentine's Day to be exact, he did something no guy had ever done before, he asked me to be his girlfriend.

He wasn't like the guys that I was used to talking to. He was different. He was sweet. And he made me feel like I was somebody.

On our first actual date as a couple, he took me to Red Lobster. He knew I loved shrimp, and that weekend, they were having endless shrimp. As I began to eat my meal, I look over and saw that all he was eating was biscuits.

"Are you going to eat anything else?" I asked

He shook his head.

I felt horrible. I thought that maybe he doesn't have enough money to pay for both of our meals, so I offered to pay. Again, he shook his head.

While leaving the restaurant I looked at him puzzled "why did you not eat anything" I asked?

"I'm allergic to Seafood and I didn't want to have an allergic reaction while we were on our first date"

And that was the day I knew I had loved him. He was one of the most selfless people I'd ever met, and he always put me first no matter the situation.

I lived in Missouri and he lived in Illinois. And although it was good 45-minute drive, he would come to see me every weekend. Sometimes just to take me to my job 5 minutes from my house.

We dated for a year when he decided to pop the question. Unfortunately, I told him no. Although he had graduated from high school a few years before me, I was still in school, so I was not ready for that.

The next year I graduated. We both moved out of our parents' house and got an apartment together. I explained to my grandmother that we were just roommates, which of course was a lie, because two months later I had to explain why my roommate and I were having a baby together.

Finding out I was pregnant was very scary for me. All the fears that I once had came rushing back into my head again. I was reminded over and over again that I wasn't supposed to get pregnant because the scars on my belly were not supposed to be able to expand that far without starting to rip.

Along with those thoughts, I had other thoughts about what my life would be like after this. I wanted to go to college. I wanted to have a big career. I felt as if I had screwed up.

How would God ever forgive me for doing this?

I spent my whole pregnancy hiding from the world. I didn't want everyone to know that I was that girl that got pregnant as a teenager. I was already judged enough; I didn't want to be judged for this too.

After 9 months of beating myself up in my head. I delivered the sweetest baby boy a week after my birthday.

The year after that, my fiancé and I decided to elope and spend the rest of our lives together.

If I told you that being married at such a young age and having a kid was easy, I would be lying. There were so many things that I had to get comfortable with. For instance, Calvin didn't know that I wore wigs when we first started to date. It wasn't until he was helping me search for something in my closet one day that he ended up finding a wig. He walked out of the closet holding it up and said: "you wear these thingies?" I had turned red in the face and shamefully said yes. I thought he would respond and think that I was weird or that he wouldn't want to date me anymore, but he just looked at me, smiled and gave me one of the biggest hugs and said I love you.

After we got married he asked me why I never walked around the house without my wigs on. I laughed and said I didn't know and changed the subject. But of course, I knew. I was still so insecure about myself. Even though I was married and I knew my husband loved me for me, I still had to get used to fully being my whole self around him.

And then there was the whole issue of gaining weight after I had the baby. There were days that I just wanted to throw in the towel. As a matter of fact, I felt like my confidence had gone down after having our baby because of the weight that I gained.

Having scars was one thing, gaining weight was another, but having scars and gaining weight at the same time felt like a lot to handle. Especially when you had family members telling you how big you had gotten and how you needed to lose weight.

It wasn't until a couple of years into our marriage that one day my son looked at me and asked me what happened to my skin, and told me that I was the most beautiful person he'd ever seen even with my burns, that I looked at my life a different way.

I decided that day: that it wasn't about what everyone else thought about me, that I was going to be me unapologetically for the rest of my life, and that I would be the best wife and mother that my family could ever imagine.

I started to work out and eat healthy. And in just a couple of months, I lost all of that weight.

It's amazing how it took the words from the mouth of a baby to make me realize what true beauty really means.

It made me realize the beauty really is in the eye of the beholder and the only thing it took for me to be beautiful was to just be myself.

CHAPTER 9

WHAT I KNOW NOW

When I started telling myself I am beautiful I start believing that I am beautiful, and the new light in which I saw myself started to influence the way others looked at me. I was asked to become a part of a really cool project a few years back and this project started off as a guy taking a picture of one of his beautiful friends who happened to be a burn survivor, to becoming a book filled with burn survivors showing their scars and sharing their stories. I was one of those survivors and being in that book (which was called *Beauty Is*) made me feel like superwoman. To this day I look at that book and see nothing but courage when I turn the pages.

No one knew except for me and my husband but I was actually pregnant with our second child, in that picture.

After two years of trying, God had finally answered our prayers. Being pregnant with our daughter was amazing. I felt good, I looked good, and life was just going really well. That was until something started happening; the thing that the doctors said would prevent me from having kids... The skin on my belly started ripping. My pregnancy became so painful that I was barely able to move without feeling like I wanted to cry. Eventually, I was put on bed rest for the rest of my pregnancy and was induced almost a month before the baby was due because of the intensity of the stretching.

Once again that was a moment that showed just how incredible our God is. When I had that baby girl, I absolutely knew that I had to keep walking in confidence. I had the privilege of having a mini-me, who I would be able to walk hand in hand with, to teach her about all loving herself.

Though it was going well, I still noticed that sometimes I was still a little insecure about certain things. So, I decided that I needed to take it up a notch. One day, while sitting on the couch I told myself that it was time for me to be brave. And with that, I uploaded a YouTube video of me talking about the fire and for the first time in my life, I took off my wig for the world to see. I still had my wig cap on in that video, but that was still a huge step for me. It took me a few hours to actually push that upload button, and when I did I felt free. It was as if a breath of fresh air hit me. At that moment in my life, I no longer felt like a prisoner. Everything I ever felt insecure about was now out.

The responses I got after that post was simply touching. Who would have thought that just being 100% you would touch so many lives?

That video led me to several speaking engagements where I was able to share with others my story and inspire them to live confidently no matter what.

If you were to ask me today what confidence is, I would say confidence is being at peace with exactly who you are right now. Or in other words, being fearlessly you.

I will also tell you that I still don't have it all figured out, and that it's okay that we continue to learn and grow each and every day.

Here are a few steps that you can take towards fearlessly being you.

1.   Get out of your head. Get rid of all the negative thoughts you have running through your head. Be very aware of self-talk. Whenever you catch yourself thinking or saying something negative about yourself, switch it around. If you're always telling yourself

that you aren't good enough or you aren't pretty or smart enough, you'll start to become exactly what you are saying. Your mind can only think one thought at a time, so changing the negative into a positive simply eliminates the negative.

2.   Surround yourself with positive people. I know you may have heard this a billion times but the people you hang with really do matter. It's time to really consider getting rid of those people in your lives that intentionally put you down and lower your confidence.

3.   Believe in yourself. No one can believe in you the way you need to

believe in yourself. You must convince yourself that you have what it takes to achieve everything you have set your mind upon.

4. Ignore what others think of you. We are constantly worried about what everyone else is thinking of us. Here's a secret; most of the time no one is thinking about you. They are too busy thinking about their own lives. And you know what? If they are thinking of you, they are wondering what you are thinking of them.

5. Love yourself for who you are. You are beautifully and wonderfully made. You will be amazed

SCARLESS

at what God can do through your uniqueness when you give it to Him. Start praying and ask God to help you accept yourself exactly the way you are.

With finding my confidence, I went from being a little girl scared to come out of the house to being someone who is brave enough to share her deepest insecurities to the world, to inspire everyone else to find their own confidence. I am now a wife and a mother, I sit on the board of directors of the burn camp I once attended, I am a speaker and officially an author.

I was once told that if I wasn't burned I could have been a model and on the cover of a magazine one day. Well, guess what? I am a model. I'm God's model, I'm my child's model, I'm my own model. I have a purpose for my life and so do you. No matter what you go through in life I want you to know that you are you, and that's what makes you beautiful. Remember this one thing, you are not your scars (inside or out) so no matter how many scars you have gotten along the way, you can still come out SCARLESS.

ABOUT THE AUTHOR

About the Author: After being burned and overcoming low self-esteem Kanisha Anthony is known for inspiring others to love themselves in the skin their in. While recently growing a big following by showing pictures of her scars Kanisha use's her platform to share her story and encourage others along the way. Kanisha is a wife and mother of three. She is an entrepreneur and sits on the board of directors for Burns Recovered/Midwest Children's Burn Camp. Ultimately Kanisha's goal is to help others who have low self-esteem become more confident and become free of insecurities

www.kanishaAnthony.com

Made in the USA
Columbia, SC
11 April 2018